Written by Bobbie Hamsa
Illustrated by Donna Catanese

Children's Press®
A Division of Scholastic Inc.
New York • Toronto • London • Auckland • Sydney
Mexico City • New Delhi • Hong Kong
Danbury, Connecticut

For my #1 super hero
— D.C.

Reading Consultants
Linda Cornwell
Literacy Specialist

Katharine A. Kane
Education Consultant
(Retired, San Diego County Office of Education and
San Diego State University)

Library of Congress Cataloging-in-Publication Data

Hamsa, Bobbie.
    Dirty Larry / written by Bobbie Hamsa ; illustrated by Donna Catanese.
        p. cm. — (Rookie reader)
    Summary: No matter what he does, Larry always gets dirty—except in
the shower.
    ISBN 0-516-22668-1 (lib. bdg.)   0-516-27493-7 (pbk.)
    [1. Cleanliness—Fiction. 2. Stories in rhyme.] I. Catanese, Donna, ill. II.
Title. III. Series.
PZ8.3.H189 Di 2002
[E] —dc21   2001008377

CHILDREN'S PRESS, AND A ROOKIE READER®, and associated logos are trademarks and or
registered trademarks of Grolier Publishing Co., Inc. SCHOLASTIC and associated logos
are trademarks and or registered trademarks of Scholastic Inc.
    2 3 4 5 6 7 8 9 10 R 11 10 09 08 07 06

Dirty Larry gets dirty
no matter where he goes.

3

Dirty fingers.
Dirty hands.

Dirty face.

Dirty clothes.

Dirty feet.
Dirty seat.

Dirty knees.
Dirty nose.

Dirty eyes.
Dirty ears.

Dirty neck.

17

Dirty toes.

**Dirty Larry gets dirty
no matter what the hour.**

21

The only time Larry's clean
is when he's in the shower.

WORD LIST (32 WORDS)

clean	he	nose
clothes	he's	only
dirty	hour	seat
ears	in	shower
eyes	is	the
face	knees	time
feet	Larry	toes
fingers	Larry's	what
gets	matter	when
goes	neck	where
hands	no	

ABOUT THE AUTHOR

Bobbie Hamsa was born and raised in Nebraska and has a Bachelor of Arts degree in English Literature. She has worked as a copywriter for print, radio, and television, and has also written many children's books.

ABOUT THE ILLUSTRATOR

Donna Catanese lives in Cleveland, Ohio, with her husband, Joe, who is also an artist. They have two Siamese cats, Christopher and Cleo, who think that they are artists, too. She hopes that you have as much fun reading this book as she had creating the pictures!